The Moon Book

by Layne deMarin

Consultant:
Adria F. Klein, PhD
California State University, San Bernardino

CAPSTONE PRESS
a capstone imprint

Wonder Readers are published by Capstone Press,
1710 Roe Crest Drive, North Mankato, Minnesota 56003.
www.capstonepub.com

Books published by Capstone Press are manufactured with paper
containing at least 10 percent post-consumer waste.

Library of Congress Cataloging-in-Publication Data
DeMarin, Layne.
  The moon book / Layne DeMarin.—1st ed.
    p. cm.—(Wonder readers)
  Includes index.
  ISBN 978-1-4296-8636-5 (library binding)
  ISBN 978-1-4296-7942-8 (paperback)
  1. Moon—Juvenile literature. I. Title.
  QB582.D46 2012
  523.3—dc23   2011022013

Summary: Simple text and color photos introduce readers to basic information about the moon,
its phases, and how humans have explored it.

Note to Parents and Teachers

The Wonder Readers: Science series supports national science standards. These
titles use text structures that support early readers, specifically with a close photo/
text match and glossary. Each book is perfectly leveled to support the reader at
the right reading level, and the topics are of high interest. Early readers will gain
success when they are presented with a book that is of interest to them and is
written at the appropriate level.

Printed in the United States of America in North Mankato, Minnesota.
102011   006405CGS12

Table of Contents

Our Moon

The moon is Earth's closest neighbor in space. At night, it is the brightest object in our sky. It is brighter than any other star or planet.

A long time ago, people looked up
and wondered about the moon.
They didn't know much about it.
Some people thought the moon was
a goddess who lived in the sky.

Moon Shine

Now we know much more about the moon than we used to. We know that the moon shines because it **reflects** light from the sun.

The moon cannot make its own light at all. The light shining from the moon is really coming from the sun. The moon reflects sunlight.

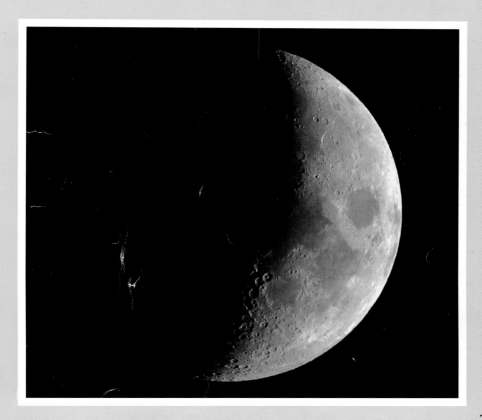

Phases of the Moon

Sometimes we can only see a thin curve of the moon. This happens when most of the sun's light hits the side of the moon facing away from Earth.

Sometimes the moon shines so brightly you can easily find your way at night. This is because the sun is shining on the side of the moon facing Earth.

Sun

Sunlight

Moon

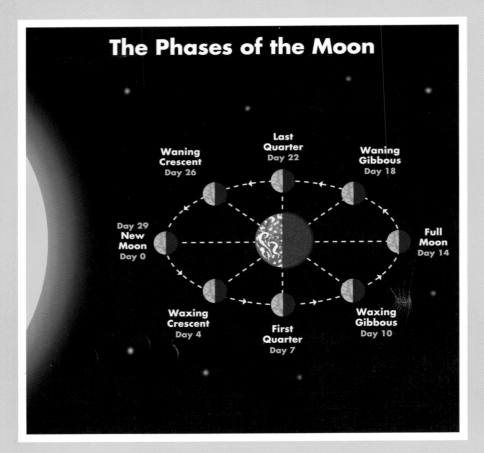

The Phases of the Moon

We also know that the moon circles, or **orbits**, Earth. It takes about one month for the moon to make one trip around Earth.

During each month, the moon goes through all of its **phases**. Each phase makes the moon look like a different shape in the sky.

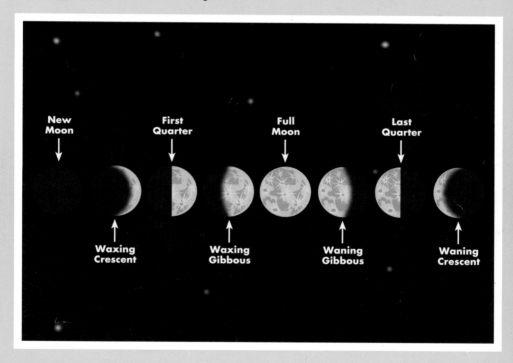

Life on the Moon

The moon is made of dust, dirt, and rocks. It has hills and valleys. It also has big holes called **craters**. Sometimes shadows on the moon's surface can make it look like the moon has a face. This is what people mean when they talk about "the man in the moon."

Of course, there is no man who lives on the moon. There is no wind or water on the moon either. It is not possible for plants or animals of any kind to live there.

It is possible for humans to visit the moon, though. In 1969, the first **astronauts** landed on the moon. They took pictures and collected moon rocks to bring back to Earth.

Astronauts have to wear special suits on the moon. The suits protect them from the blazing hot temperatures there during the day and the freezing cold temperatures at night.

These special suits also keep the astronauts from floating away into space. The moon does not have as much **gravity** as Earth does. If you jump on the moon, you could jump as high as the top of a tree!

Some day, scientists might build space stations on the moon. Astronauts could stop there to rest and refuel as they travel to other planets. Maybe you will be able to visit the moon yourself!

Glossary

astronaut	a person who travels in space
craters	deep holes on the surface of a planet
gravity	the force that pulls objects down toward the surface of a planet
orbits	travels in a circle around something, such as a planet
phases	the different shapes the moon goes through
reflects	bounces off, like the sun's light on the moon

Now Try This!

Work in pairs to write questions about the moon that can be answered in this book. Then exchange questions with another pair of students. Look through the book to find the answers to the other students' questions. Next, write questions about the moon that cannot be answered in this book. Exchange these questions with another pair of students. Do research in the library to answer these new questions.

Internet Sites

FactHound offers a safe, fun way to find Internet sites related to this book. All of the sites on FactHound have been researched by our staff.

Here's all you do:

Visit *www.facthound.com*

Type in this code: 9781429686365

Check out projects, games and lots more at
www.capstonekids.com

Index

Editorial Credits
Maryellen Gregoire, project director; Mary Lindeen, consulting editor; Gene Bentdahl, designer;
    Sarah Schuette, editor; Wanda Winch, media researcher; Eric Manske, production specialist

Photo Credits
© Josephine Wall. All Rights Reserved, 5; Digital Vision (Getty Images), 14; NASA: 15, 16, NASA: Johnson
Space Center, 12, 13; NASA: Painting by Les Bossinas (ERC, Inc.), 17; Shutterstock: Danshutter, 6, Goran
Cakmazovic, 7, Ivica Jandrijevic, 4, Lambros Kazan, 1, TRyburn, cover, Viktar Malyshchyts, 8

Word Count: **434**   Guided Reading Level: **L**   Early Intervention Level: **20**